#Triggerwarning:

Powerful Prayers for Traumatic Experiences

by 

Malandie Winston

Editor: Anthony Ambrogio

Cover Design: SOS Graphic Designs

Publisher: G Publishing LLC

ISBN: 979-8-9894404-1-2

Library of Congress Control Number: 2024902235

Published and Printed in the United States of America

#Triggerwarning:

Powerful Prayers for Traumatic Experiences

by

Malandie Winston

In memory of Gertrude, Clinton, Annie, Unis, Reggie, and Walter. Your Sacrifices have laid the foundation for all I will do and whom I will continue to be.

Words can't express my gratitude and never will. Thank you from the depths of my soul for teaching me and setting me out on my path. Your contributions to me and my family can never be repaid; they were absolutely priceless. Thank you.

Your baby girl, Mel.

Dedications i

Preface xix

Prayer For Covering 1

Superwoman 4

Prayer for Understanding 10

Over Time: Rough Touch, Molestation 14

Prayer for Self Love 19

Trap House Run 22

Prayer For the Mind 27

Crazy Tate 31

Prayer for Grace and Mercy 40

The Shot (Davie & Demarcus) 42

Prayer for my Enemies 50

Falling Love 54

Prayer for Guidance 68

Bittersweet Dad 70

Last Prayer: Thanks 101

Malandie Winston

Dedications

The truth is I don't really want to write this book. I honestly thought it could be a more simple process, but it's not. I wanted to be able to inspire and motivate while informing and giving wisdom that other young women and young men can understand and relate to but I've also created a place where I'm uncomfortable and my heart is showing. After all I've been through, I really just want my story to be a blessing to someone who's suffering through trauma. I don't like showing what pain my heart feels, because it's deep and it's dark. The truth is I'm naked before you, hoping you don't see me. The truth is there's no way to tell you this story without showing you who I am in every way and hoping that parts of me will represent parts of you. I hope that, if I'm transparent about everything I experienced, you will know how to get through to your healing too. While writing this book, I thought about the things I've experienced and the people I've known in my life—especially those who inspired me to continue my journey of life. There are times I wanted to give up, but these people help me to maintain parts of my sanity so I can continue to live a life worthy of a legacy.

*****

I want to thank my mother, Debbie, first and foremost. She went through so much to raise me and to turn me into the young lady or the Queen I am today. She showed me that you can be strong, you can be weak, you can be even misunderstood—but never give up on yourself and never give up on your family. Her determination to keep her girls together and to make them into the Queen they are today is the greatest inspiration I've known in my life. Her sacrifices, her pain, and her sorrow often quilted the tapestry that made the fabric of her daughters and the lives they now have. I'm forever grateful for every sacrifice. Through thick and thin, she has always been my best friend.

*****

I'd also like to thank my father, Kenny, who often was a mystery to me growing up. I often misunderstood who he was but always had a fear of asking him more about himself. I think that, because he was my daddy, I didn't want to question any of his decisions or reasons for any of the things he had to do or had to sacrifice to keep me in his life. He and I have had great times and we had sad times, and we've even had times when we weren't so happy with each other. But I'm extremely grateful for the strong, enduring, and humble man who is my father. Over the years, he showed me how a real man should treat a woman. I'm grateful for all his sacrifice, even the ones I didn't see but I know took place. I know I'm always going to be his Wild Child, and that's okay with me. The art of rebellion turned me into one of his greatest compositions. I'm grateful he's the most amazing God I've ever known today.

*****

I also want to recognize my sisters. I have three. Each of them brings to me something special. Each of them gives me something important that continues to keep me going.

- To my oldest sister, Val: your understanding nature and wisdom always help me to make the best decisions. You're often my confirmation, and there are times when you've been the ear to hear when I felt no one else was listening

- To my middle sister, Vee: you gave me two of the greatest gifts I will ever have in my life, my nephews. Each one is so special and so unique, and I see many parts of all of us in them. My life became amazing when they came into it. I thank you for blessing me with the opportunity to be their aunt. we may not always get along, and we may not always see things the same way, but you are truly a ride-or-die. You truly give life to the word *fighter*. I'm proud of all your accomplishments, and I know you have still yet more to give to the world.

- To my baby sister, LaLa: you, too, have given me amazing gifts of my niece and my nephew. They are my happy place, my place of joy and solace when things get hard and I find myself in pain from everything that's happening to me. You were the first reason that I changed things in my life so that I could be a better sister and a better friend and a better Father Figure, seeing that your father didn't want to stay around. Thank you for letting me play his role in your life. It's been an honor to play the part. I'm so proud of the mother that you have become. I hope and pray that, one day, when I have an opportunity to give birth I'm as loving, gentle, kind, and good-natured as you are with your babies and the babies at the daycare who love who you are. I pray that I can be as kind and attentive as you are with your babies. You will always be my baby sister, and there's absolutely nothing you can do about it. I will continue to boss you around and drive you nuts and make you smile when it's applicable. I wish you all

#Triggerwarning

the happiness in the world. You truly deserve it.

*****

Also on this journey I've been blessed to have amazing Godbrothers and Godsisters. There are so many of you that I cannot name each of you one by one, but you know who you are, and you know the place that you have in my heart. Each of you has presented me with things that help me become a happier, healthier Queen.

Among all of my Godbrothers, special mention must be made of Gared, Terry, Anthony, and Thomas. You have been the quintessential Brotherhood I've needed. You watch out for me, and you always aim to protect me. You also let me know when I'm wrong and congratulate me when I'm right, and even sometimes scare me into acting better. I thank you for loving me for years, even at times when I wasn't at my best. Even through my sickness Jared, you have been an amazing helping hand. Thank you for caring for me and for my mother when it is needed. Thank you for always being my protector—especially when I wasn't able to protect myself.

*****

Mr. Levine, thank you for all the years you loved me and cared for me and my entire family. Your sacrifices changed our lives forever. You helped me to acquire my first home, and you helped me and my family to get the health care we needed. You took us out of a bad situation and put us into a good one, all because of our love for each other and our love of the God we serve. I want you to know that, more than anything, you affected my relationship with God, and I'm so grateful that I could be able to give you, from me, what I thought you needed as well. And thank you for believing in me and my business and being the first person to invest in it when no one else believed in what I was trying to do. The fact that you gave me the start-up money even when I didn't really believe in my own dream says so much about who you really are. I wish every happiness and joy and overwhelming prosperity for your life and in the lives of those you still aim to help.

*****

On this journey I've also had new people come along and show me a different way of moving through all my changes. One of the greatest changes in my life has been me being able to go and get therapy for all the

x

things that I've experienced and all the pain I've gone through.

My therapist, Vicki; my psychologist, Dionne; and my spiritual therapist, Smith—you changed my life so much. I had wanted help for years because I knew that all my need to harm or to get out of life wasn't a good thing. It wasn't a healthy thing, but I knew it had something to do with everything that I saw in my life, and I just needed a way to express it and get it out and try to work through my emotions about it. I came to you with a blank canvas ready to be filled with information, color, and writing. Thank you so much for taking the time to write on the paper—the canvas of my life. Dionne, you are absolutely a Healer in understanding individuals who struggle with Mental Health. It's such a beautiful way to bless the world.

#Triggerwarning

Thank you for always teaching me new ways to elevate my thoughts and to alleviate my pain. Thank you for knowing that I wanted to be better than what I was and I wanted to be able to heal from all the turmoil I had been in and all the pain I have felt. Thank you for allowing me to be myself. Thank you for always reaching out to help me when I was in need. You have been an absolute bright spot in my life, and, even though I know I won't be able to spend forever coming to see you, I'm grateful for whatever time we continue to have together. You've been a very beautiful and amazing ambassador of change.

*****

To Vicky: I always love our talks. You know when I'm not myself, and I'm grateful that you were able to see and understand I

Malandie Winston

needed more than what I was getting in life. You decided to give that to me. I love the stories we share, and I love the information and wisdom that you put inside of me. It has changed my life for the better. Every time you give me homework or exercises, I feel as if I'm in school again, and I'm so excited to learn not just about myself but about what can make me greater than I already am.

Thank you for challenging me and not letting me give up on myself and not letting me be a victim. You are truly a manifestor of survivors, Vicky. Thank you so much.

*****

To the pastor at the clinic: you know who you are. I wanted to tell you that it is so amazing that you were able to take the word of God and apply it to my mental-health situation. It was the most amazing thing that

I have ever seen. I finally felt that I had the confirmation I needed to move forward and to let go of all the past hurt and pain. You are able to find my voice within the scriptures and show it to me in such a way that I can relate it to what I was feeling. Thank you for enlightening me and showing me that the scriptures are true and that I am a child of God. No matter what I go through or where I go, God will always love me.

*****

To my girl Tee: you are such an amazing friend. You are my sister, and I love you because you love me whether I'm in good or bad, whether I'm happy or sad. You love the diva in me and you put me in my place when I want to talk smack. We both love fashion so much, and we always find it fun to challenge each other with how we look.

However, the best thing of all is that I could depend on you in my time of need and you always would come through. I can't express my gratitude enough for every moment you stepped in and treated me like your sister. I am grateful for the friendship and the Sisterhood we share. I am blessed to know you.

*****

There are so many other people that I would love to talk about, and I'd love to write about what they did that has made such an impact on me from the time I was a child all the way up to my adult life. I'm grateful for each one, and I pray that whoever picks up this book and reads it will not be the same because of something they read. I want this book to be a catalyst for real conversation about trauma, especially trauma that people don't want to talk about. I want this book to be a catalyst for change in laws, in politics, and in Ministry in order to protect the people who are deeply affected by the extreme violent crimes against women and men. I want to be the person who's able to show someone else how to find their healing.

Young lady or young man reading this book, I want you to know that you are not alone and that, despite all the problems you've dealt with and all the Pain you have endured, none of it was a mistake—no, it was more of a transition to help you become exactly who you're becoming right now.

This book is your safe place. These written words are your confirmation that your pain is real because my pain was real, and I felt it, and I went through it, and I still deal with it day to day. I need you to know that someone out there loves you, and it's not a joke; it's not a cliché. There are people who would love to have you in their life, and, right now, I hope that you're led to them, and I hope that you are led to the Avenues that help you to find your healing and your Solace and Peace again. Just because you're a victim doesn't mean you can't become the victor; it just means you've got plenty of time to originate the person you claim to be in your future.

This book is dedicated to every survivor from every trauma. You are needed in this world. We don't want you to leave it without sharing your story. I hope that this book will push you to tell your story. I hope that this book will push you to show and tell your truth. Even if it hurts to say it out loud, it's time that you just say it. I'm here from you.

I'm one of you. I Shall Overcome. This book is my labor of love to each and every one of you: the little girl, the little boy, the teenager, the young adult who's trying to understand why all of this happened to them.

Let me be your voice. I'll be your safe place, and I pray that one day you can be someone else's safe place too. I remind you that there is a trigger warning for what you're about to read. Please understand I'm not telling it to make you relive anything. I'm telling it so you'll see how I was able to move forward from what I endured. I hope my transparency is an absolute blessing to your existence. Let's all move forward, never looking back. Today is a new day to live. Live it.

Malandie Winston

Preface

So I guess you want me to say something that's amazing and full of grandeur, something that makes you say "Wow!" and "Really?" Well, I will only say that life is for the living and that I have *lived*."

Many people always assume that life is what you make it—a true-enough reference, but you can make life many things: the ultimate truth is that there are many roads in life. You may take three different roads, but you always just end up on one road. It's the journey that matters.

At this point in my life, I have had some time to reflect, as most people do, and look deeply at my decisions, the pursuit of happiness, the trials and tribulations, the mountains and the valleys, and the starts and finishes. I have come to one and only one decision—that every one of those moments sculpted me into the very Queen I am today. Each moment is different in its content, each with many animated characters who play obvious and not-so-obvious roles. Each moment has its climax, turning point, and duration—and, most of all, if you are lucky, you will have an ending, a conclusion, a finale.

Our lives are a novel, a trilogy, a story that's dying to spring forth and help others through their path. However, as with most great adventures, there truly never is a complete ending, since life continues. In my case, I see that—considering all I have been faced with—I am only at the beginning of my testimony, I am only at the beginning of forever.

Malandie Winston

Here it is: everything in my heart and soul. Truth is, I may have written this work in a way that may seem different, but to me it's perfect. You get the rare opportunity to see my life through my eyes. I am a blowing kite; I flow with the wind where it leads me. I am a tree; I grow where the gardener plants me. I am deep blue water; I flow throughout all the lands freely, giving to those around me. I am the writer with the vision that only I can see but aim to bring to life in the mind of the reader who reads.

Allow me the pleasure of telling my truth. I walk this path alone but safe, remembering that, when things become hard and become unbearable, it is in those moments that God has carried me. My heavenly father has pulled me through so much. Father God has allowed me the ability to share my tribulations and trials with you in such a profound and personal way. God has always saved me, no matter what, and each story is another opportunity for the reader to see God's greatness in the details.

How blessed I am to have the chance to tell the truth of how I've felt all of this time. It's been a blessing to open my heart to the world and have it heard. The power of one's spirit surpasses the power of the pen, but it's true that the one needs the other. Through my writing, you also will realize the power of prayer when it's used for the greater good. There's no way anyone could survive the trauma I've endured without someone praying on their behalf. You will see the power of the soul when faced with adversity. How do you overcome your fears? Simple, you face them. I know that true strength lies in each one of us, and we each have the power through Christ to overcome. This is just my way of sharing my trauma with you in hopes it helps you deal with yours.

This book is my dedication to God above for letting me pass through my struggles without them breaking the soul he gave unto me. God has been my constant friend, companion, first love—he's the joy of my life. He truly is the wind beneath my wings. I would be nothing without his grace and mercy. There are obstacles I would have never faced if God hadn't given me the strength to push forward, never looking back. He held my hand through every situation. I will always praise him in all that I do. I thank him for all I have become. Amen.

This book is also dedicated to people who have faced grave opposition with a humble and genuine manner, those who have seen that the rainbow has an end and that there is no sorrow heaven cannot heal. This book is made in honor of every person who has realized they are important in the material of the world, and that with perseverance and determination all dreams and aspirations can and will be realized.

This book is dedicated to you, the reader, who finds inspiration, takes it. and molds it into your own dream. Never be afraid to step outside of your boundaries. Take what belongs to you. There are no chains on your destiny; there are no holds on your faith. You can be free from the trauma. You too can write your story and help others to heal through you. You can indeed change the world, but, more importantly, you can change the way you view the tapestry of the world. Allow this book to help you realize you are never alone and that, in this world, Malandie believes in your ability to overcome your hurt and pain and finally find your peace and joy. You will be happy again. Trust me. It will not be easy, and it indeed will take time, but you will see better days.

I truly hope that, after reading my story, you will want to also share yours. Thank you for reading my life. Thank God for saving my life time and time again. I'm just blessed to have this moment and share it with all of you.

Throughout the book, you will see prayers that I said to help me on my journey. I pray that these prayers will do for you what they did for me. Prayer is my divine love language, and I share some of my deepest prayers with all of you. Let my prayers be a light to the dark places in your journey. We all will feel joy and happiness again. It's possible; I'm living, breathing proof that God truly saves. I am a miracle, and you are, too. Never forget it; never take it for granted.

Breathe; your moment of clarity has arrived. Don't give up on yourself.

"Be not a judge of men, but instead be a platform for the changes of man: change is what life is all about, change is what makes each of us who we are. Keep growing; keep changing. You're almost there"

– Malandie W

Prayer For Covering

Dear Father,

I lift my face to you and humble myself before your presence. I am just a slow servant and need your love to survive. I know that you care about my life, and I ask that you cover me with your love and safety. I ask that you cover my life with your holy spirit. I ask that you lead me in the right direction in life. Please, Father, give me clarity for the road ahead. Father, guide my every step. Give me the heart to work through my issues so I may be closer to you, Father, even more.

Father, send me where I need to be in life. I ask you to let your holy word saturate my soul. Allow your word to be my guide. I ask, Father, that you keep me and all I love safe. Let no harm come to your beloved children. Cover us in your love and light. Be a light to our path. Guide us even when we are caught in the dark. Father, give us the opportunity to love you right. Give us a word of praise. Let us always want your will to be done. Cover my home and cover my car when I travel. Cover always my life and family. Cover my family and friends and send angelic protection around them all. Keep me safe at all times. Thank you, Father, for being my everything. I trust you always.

AMEN

Superwoman

It had been a great weekend, and my aunt and uncle were well on their way, taking me home. I was about seven years old. I had spent the entire weekend with them while my mother was working. It had been so great. We went to Carowinds Amusement Park and then to a family cookout and then to church. But I was always super happy when I got to go home to my mother.

We were getting close to the apartment where we stayed in the projects. Even though it wasn't the richest of places, it had the richest treasure of people there, full of the shouts of kids who were always playing outside and the aroma of barbecues that people were always cooking on their porches. I always noticed the kids riding their bicycles. I loved how their hair flowed in the wind; hence my admiration for shiny straight hair like a Barbie doll's. I loved hair blowing in the wind; it seemed so freeing to me. I loved my home, and, more than that, I loved my mother.

Once we pulled up, my uncle began to get my bags from the trunk and unpack all the toys and games I had won over the weekend. Then my aunt, who was so lovely, got out of the car and helped me put my sweater on. It was chilly outside but not too bad; the summer was so lovely when it was like this. I jumped out of the car and was suited, and then we began our walk to the door. All I could think was school tomorrow and my mommy: *Wait till she sees what I've won.*

#Triggerwarning

We got to the house where I stayed and walked to the door, but something didn't seem quite right. This feeling of anxiety fell into the pit of my stomach. I asked my aunt why there was glass on the ground near our front door. She didn't respond, and my uncle decided we wouldn't knock but just walk into the house, stepping carefully over the glass.

I remember it all as if it happened yesterday. Outside in our mini garden all the flowers were smashed. Inside, the house was a mess. The tv was on. *Superman* was playing—not the current *Superman* but the original with Christopher Reeve; it was one of my favorite movies.

My mom was sitting quietly, staring straight at the tv. As I got closer to her, I asked, "Mama, what's wrong? Are you okay?" She said nothing

That's when I noticed the one thing that stayed with me the rest of my life. The blood. There was blood coming from my mother's ears and from her head. I started to panic and cry. I was so scared—"What has happened to my mother? Why is she bleeding?"—why wasn't I home to protect her?

Soon my aunt and uncle took over. They asked her what happened. At first she wouldn't respond or say anything. Then her silence broke. She told us that a strange man had knocked on her door, claiming he wanted to sell something, but in reality he was trying to rob our house.

He grabbed my mother in an attempt to get in, but to no avail. My mother said she hit him over the head with a glass bottle that happened to be on the porch, and then he took the same bottle and hit my mother with it.

My aunt and uncle wanted to know more, but all my mom kept asking was, "Would you please call the police?" She was still in shock and not really speaking coherently.

Eventually she stood up, and the extent of her injury quickly revealed itself. The blood just poured out of my mother's ear and head, and we knew we had to get her to the hospital quickly. My uncle decided he would take her to the hospital and he helped us get all the glass up that was at the front door.

I had to deal with all kinds of thoughts that day. I wondered how scared my mother must have been when her life was threatened. I wondered what went through her mind when he attacked her. What if we hadn't come when we did? What else could have happened?

The situation had traumatized me and my mother both, and it definitely scared my uncle and aunt. I was so grateful that day that my mom was okay. She survived such a scary ordeal. I'm just glad she walked away with only stitches. She was my own personal superwoman.

Prayer for Understanding

Dear Father God above,

I'm reaching out to you with my heart on my sleeve. Father, I am lying before you in pain, praying for a miracle. I am seeking to understand why others have hurt me so badly. What have I done, Father, to deserve it?

Father, show me how you need me to be. Help me to make peace with the things I don't even understand. Help me to see the light even when I feel I am covered in darkness. Help me to see love where I only see pain. Father, guide my heart to be closer to healing. Help me to be kind even when I don't want to be. I ask you to give clarity where chaos once stood. Help me to learn your will and your way for me. Help me be better each day.

Father, guide my thoughts and guide my life. I know that what has been done to me is not your will or your way; help me heal from the inside out. Every touch I felt that was against your will, let it die away from me. Father, heal the person who chooses to harm me; heal their mind and their heart. I rebuke the spirit of perversion and lust in Jesus ' holy name. I shall stand strong, even when I feel like giving up. I shall overcome this adversity. My soul is in your care.

I trust you, Father, to heal my mental and physical injuries completely. I trust you for healing my mind of everything that is not like you. I love you, Father; you are great, I live to please you always.

amen

Over Time: Rough Touch, Molestation

When I was younger, starting from the time I was eight until I was about 12 or 13, I was a victim of sexual abuse. It happened over and over with a family member that I trusted deeply. At the time, I thought this behavior was normal, that it was what all family members do. I found out later in life that it was definitely *not* normal.

It started off as gentle little quick touches. Slight hands on the thigh or a caress on my shoulder when no one was around. This is why parents should never leave older kids alone with younger kids without supervision. He would say, "I like your skin, fam; it's very soft," then blow a kiss or kiss me on my arm.

Each time, he would go a little further, do a little more. He would touch my vaginal area and insert his fingers into my anus. Then, other times, he would be cold—no touches at all—making me think I did something wrong.

Sometimes we would look at pornos of people doing it on tv, and he would tell me to watch. He liked to watch porno all the time when no one was around. He would sneak and find those videos. I really didn't understand what sex was, so, when I saw people climax, I found it disgusting.

I didn't like when he would finger me because it gave me weird butterflies in my tummy. I would often tell him, "Stop!" and he would say, "Just a little bit more." Sometimes my booboo would hurt from how rough he would rub it. I don't think anyone knew he was slowly torturing my mind.

One time he let one of his friends touch me in my booboo. I had a hard time letting the other boy touch me because i wasn't used to him. They tried sticking things in me, causing me pain, but it wouldn't work. I was a virgin and found the manipulation extremely painful. He eventually gave up. These episodes often made me feel dirty.

I always felt it was our little secret. I really was so confused about it all, but I knew that, if adults were not around it, was going to keep happening. However, as I got older, the touching was turning into more rough things, and I started to realize something was wrong with my family. To avoid this unwanted attention and abuse, I started hanging around more adults and would go along with the other kids.

Finally, after being touched time and again, I finally had enough and threatened to tell everyone, He was so shocked and scared that he immediately stopped.

I continued to see him at family gatherings and often would speak with him because I didn't like the awkward feelings between us. But, in the depths of my mind, I knew he wanted me to be his toy. I was so afraid it would happen to others, but, instead of saying anything, I remained silent because I wanted to keep the family together. I felt, if I said something, it would destroy the only happiness I ever knew and loved.

I still have nightmares about it. I still wonder if he did to others what he'd done to me. Did someone hurt him, and that's why he hurt me? I guess I will never know. However, I do know he *still* shows signs of liking me in a non-family way. Absolutely disgusting. I just don't get why anyone would do that to their family. Why me? Why them? My soul is already torn.

Malandie Winston

Prayer for Self Love

Dear Father up above,

It is your humble servant coming to you with my deep secret. I secretly don't love myself and want so desperately to do so. Father, I have been broken and hurt, used and mistreated. I have seen so much in my short time here on the place we call Earth.

Father, when I look in the mirror, I don't see what I should. I ask, Father, that you change my heart to change my mind. I ask that everyone who said something hurtful be forgiven because they know not what they do. I ask you to also help them to heal just as you are healing me. I ask, Father, that I learn to smile from the inside out and my joy becomes a constant and not a fading trend. Father, I beg you to heal every unholy part of me. I ask for your guidance and clarity in all things.

Teach me, Father, to love the person I see in the mirror. I am not less than but I am greater. Father, keep me focused on your will and your way. Help me to not be so hard on myself. Keep me always forever in your presence. Help me not to hate myself and not to hate others. Keep me always under the protection of your heavenly host.

I am glad that I am yours and you are mine. I pray, when I look in the mirror, that I will see you, Father, smiling back at me because I was made in your image. I am your child. I want your love always. AMEN

Trap House Run

During the time I was rolling with Davie and Demarcus, this new guy from Jersey moved into the neighborhood. Hason seemed like an okay type of guy, but he also seemed like he might cause trouble for people. Well, of course he befriended Davie and Demarcus so he could get all the smoke he wanted. So, even though Davie was keeping an eye on him, he was still making his cash.

One day, Davie came to me and asked me to take a bag to Hason. I agreed, grabbed the bag, and went out as I normally would.

I knocked on Hason's door, and his younger brother let me in. He told me his brother would be out soon. Once Hason came out of his bedroom, he asked me for the bag, and then he had his brother give me the cash. Everything seemed pretty simple.

Then, as I was about to walk off, Hason asked me if I would like something to eat or if I wanted to stay and play video games with them.

I told him no thanks, and he chuckled.

He then proceeded to grab my wrist and ask me again, "Are you gonna give a Negro a shot or what?"

I gently said, " I'm not really interested in that, but thank you anyway."

Now he was blocking the doorway and asked me another time, "When you gonna give a Negro some pussy?"

I was taken back, but I wasn't afraid until I noticed him grabbing something.

His brother then jumped up and told Hason, "What the hell you thinking, my nigga? She said *no*."

Hason pushed his brother out of the way and started shooting at me.

I was running fast as hell with heels on. He shot a second time. I fell down the front door steps and jumped up, still running, and he shot at me again.

By this point I wasn't even looking behind me. I was just running as fast as my legs could take me.

As I approached the corner of the apartment where Davie could see me, Hason got off one more shot. I was running full speed at Davie, who had a look of confusion on his face until I explained what happened.

Davie wasn't happy with what he heard. He told me he and Demarcus would handle it. I remember thinking how lucky I was to escape all those shots just because I wouldn't give a guy some play. I couldn't wrap my head around it. About a week later, the cops busted Hason on some other charg. Davie told me they got a tip that Hason was a fugitive from New Jersey, where the police had been looking for him because he had been assaulting and raping young women and girls.

I remember telling Davie, "I wonder who told on him…"

I'll never forget Davie's response. He said, "Nobody will ever help a nigga keeping other niggas down; he deserves to rot in prison."

We never saw Hason or his little brother again. He knew it wasn't safe after he shot at me. Jamaicans are territorial. Period.

Malandie Winston

Prayer For the Mind

Dear Father above,

I lay before you asking that you help me to be better. I ask that you may heal me in every area of my life that isn't whole. I ask, Father, that you heal my brokenness and the parts of me that glorify you. I ask, Father, that you lay your hands on me. Heal all of me—my heart and my mind. I ask that you renew my mind and give me guidance on this road we call life. I ask you to clear up every unclean thought and break every unclean action. Show me myself through your love. Help me to be an open vessel to your power and your way. Father, please keep me close to you and don't let me stray far. I need your love, direction, and guidance in all things. I know I'm not worthy, but I know you love all your children, and I ask you to always keep loving me. Break away every generational curse sent to take the minds of those I love.

I break every single stranglehold of mental health in your children. I break the spirits sent to sicken the mind and heart.

Father, where your children are concerned, stomp out the enemy so it will be no more. Father, send us help and guidance in our journey. Send those who want to do great in my life. Father, keep my thoughts fixed on your will and your way. Father, touch my body, my heart, and my soul. Allow your divine will to be done in my life and in the lives of others. Father, we trust you. Father, forgive us for not listening as we should. We apologize for every sin committed against your will. Father, we trust you in all things. I am blessed to always call you mine.

In Jesus' holy name,

AMEN

Malandie Winston

Crazy Tate

So my sister hated this new guy I was dating. She kept telling me, "Sister, something is not right with that guy, I don't know what it is, but he ain't right."

I would look at her and giggle and say, "You never like anyone," and proceed walking out the house to go and see Tate.

Truth is, when I met Tate, he was pleasant and very engaging with me. We would walk through the neighborhood for hours, just talking and connecting. He would tell me his family issues and how he could never see his daughter. After hearing about his life, I concluded that he needed someone to be kind to him and show him true love. I honestly felt sorry for him. I felt it was my job to be his friend and maybe even his girlfriend.

So I had been talking to him for about three weeks, and, every time I would go see him, my sister would remind me how she didn't trust him and neither should I. But what did I do but keep seeing him even after being told he wasn't a good guy.

On this particular day, I drove over to his house to hang out with him and his neighbor and play video games. He was very welcoming and asked if I had eaten yet. I told him I was okay and wouldn't be there for long. He sat on the couch beside me and began rubbing my legs and giving me a kiss on my cheek. We were all talking and having fun. Then Tate got up and went into his room, which was directly in front of the living room.

While he was in his room, his neighbor and I started chatting about the best time to be intimate with someone you just met. I said out loud, "Well, if it's real love, then they will get to know you first, and, after a couple months, intimacy could possibly start."

The neighbor yelled back, all excited, saying, "There's no way I'm waiting that long for some pussy."

I then said, "Well, I am waiting with Tate."

That's when Tate flung his door open. He stood on the threshold, upset and irritated. He looked from me to his neighbor and said, "You're planning on making me wait for months before I can get some? Hell, no!"

At this point both his neighbor and I became uncomfortable with his tone. His neighbor quickly told him, "It's just a conversation. Doesn't mean it will actually be that way, homey."

Then, for whatever reason, Tate yelled, "You not gonna do that with me! You're gonna give me what I want when I want."

The neighbor and I stood up because we both sensed a change in him. I looked at him and blurted out, "I will not sleep with any man if I don't want to." Why did I say that?

Tate turned red, and his eyes got big. He said, "You fucking lying because that ass is mine! And, if you not giving nothing up, get the fuck out my house."

I went to the door to leave, but, though I tried and tried, I couldn't get it open right away.

Tate was pissed and suddenly started charging in our direction. Infuriated, he jumped in my face, and I decided to back up out the door. I yelled, " I ain't giving you shit; you're crazy as hell! What the fuck is wrong with you?" Why did I say that?

The neighbor was holding Nate back so he couldn't charge at me. The neighbor said, "Get in your car and leave right now! He's trippin'! Run, girl."

As soon as he said that, I took off running to my car. I ran as fast as I could.

By that time, Tate had knocked the neighbor down and stepped over him, screaming and yelling all forms of profanities. He was moving fast, and I had to get to my car quickly.

As soon as I got to my car, I unlocked the doors as fast as I could. My heart was pumping fast as hell. He was right behind me. The neighbor was trying to calm him down, but he was still charging at my car.

I got in the car, but I had forgotten I had left my windows down, and, as soon as Tate got to my car, he put his arm through my window, trying to grab me.

The neighbor kept yelling, "Girl, crank your car and get the hell out of here." I fiddled with my keys trying to put them into the ignition. Finally, I had the car running and began rolling up all my windows. I was crying and screaming, telling Tate to get away from my car.

He jumped on my hood and tried to break my windows, but I hit the gas hard and fast and got away.

I was scared. I lived right down the street from him. What if he came back to my house to finish the argument. I was so scared when I got home that I talked to no one but went straight to my room and just cried.

Why had he lost it like that? I didn't get it at all, but I definitely was sure of one thing: what my sister had told me was right. He wasn't right. For the next week, I had no contact with Tate, but I saw him walking past my home.

I was very sure I would never see him again. Or that's what I thought. But one day my sister and I were watching the daily news, and suddenly the reporter started talking about this random shooting at the movie theater. I wasn't prepared for what I saw next. Tate's picture appeared on the news; he was arrested for killing his pregnant sister's boyfriend.

It sent chills down my spine. My sister looked at me and said, "I told you something was wrong with that guy, and now he is locked up for murder." She just shook her head.

I then realized how God was protecting me even when I didn't realize. I looked up at my sister and told her, "When me and Tate went walking some weeks back, he told me his sister's boyfriend had been beating her and that, if he found out the guy ever hit her again, he would kill him."

My sister looked at me in a way that said *That could have been you*. We both were thinking that. Why had I not listened to her? Why did I have this need in me to help every bird with broken wings

Everything isn't for everyone. This definitely could have gone a lot different. God truly had protected me. A few weeks later, I received a letter from Tate, who was in jail awaiting trial. He sent several letters.

Him pleading that I take him back. I took each one and threw it away. I had learned my lesson. Don't entertain CRAZY.

Prayer for Grace and Mercy

Father God,

I reach out to you in the time of trial asking that you see past my flaws and my shortcomings and love me even more. I ask that you send your grace and mercy to cover me, and to keep me from all hurt, harm, or danger. I may not yet be in the place you would have me, but I am your child and trust you, Father, with my life. I ask that you keep me safe and show me my enemies so

I can pray for their salvation. I ask that you help me to discern that which belongs to me and what doesn't belong to me. I don't deserve your love and care, but you give it nonetheless. Please allow my eyes to be open and my ears to hear at all times. Let every spirit sent to destroy me be destroyed and stomped out in Jesus' holy name. I am your child, and I trust your love.

AMEN

The Shot (Davie & Demarcus)

The truth is I had always hung around those who liked to make money. I was a girl who wanted to be a business woman so badly. So I always put myself around hustlers and business owners when I could.

I will admit I had my hands in some illegal things at this time in my life. I was in a survival mood. My mom and her man at the time were having issues, so I was trying to be prepared by having some cash and some friends I could count on. I had been helping out my Jamaican friends, Davie and Demarcus, with some traps they had. They had no problem being my friend and helping me out when I needed help. Guys always love to have a pretty girl hanging around.

Anyway, Davie and Demarcus were the neighborhood dealers and they had a pretty simple and clean operation. That's why I always hung around them. Davie would always tell me how he separated his real life from his hustle. He was very smart and never got caught. On the other hand, Demarcus, who was quiet, liked the wrong types of women most of the time.it would always bring unwanted attention to the trap.

Demarcus and I had started to talk to each other but never put any titles on it because of the lifestyle he was living. Neither brother wanted to ever put me in danger. At this particular time, me and my family had an apartment right before the trap house so we all could take dirt paths from the back and around to the front to handle business. So we all got along, and everyone knew what was the deal.

One night, we three were hanging out on the neighborhood stoop. Just talking and watching cars come by to grab their goodies. Nothing special was happening. The evening air was crisp and felt amazing to me. A small breeze was blowing through the trees.

After a while, we saw an older man with dreads come down the hill, looking for some smoke. Davie told him, "We don't have any more." (Of course, I knew that was Davie's way of making sure this guy wasn't the police.

The guy didn't seem bothered. He stood in front of Demarcus and asked him for a light. This was a normal request in this lifestyle. Demarcus started to check his pockets, and so did Davie.

But the guy pulled out a gun and shot Demarcus square in the chest at point-blank range.

I remember seeing the dread run up the hill to a waiting car still shooting back at us a second time as he was running. That's when Davie pulled out his gun and began shooting, but the others were fast and had already pulled out immediately after shots were fired. They were long gone.

Davie and I both went to pick Demarcus up. The crazy part is we didn't see any blood, and, even after we dragged him to the trap house, all we could see was only this bullet hole right over his heart area.

I knelt down and worked on holding Demarcus, trying to keep him awake. All the while, Davie was getting rid of the drugs and stashing the cash at our apartment. I had never seen Davie move so fast. He ditched the beepers and the product so fast. I was sure he had done this before. I remember everything moving in slow motion and me thinking *Demarcus will die in my arms if EMS doesn't get here soon.*

He continued to slip between consciousness and unconsciousness. I kept slapping his face and pinching his arms, but he was getting less talkative and more quiet. Finally, I heard the ambulance pull up and was beyond grateful for them coming to help save his life. They asked their questions and stuff and began to put Demarcus on a stretcher. They concluded he was bleeding internally. He finally had closed his eyes, but he was safe, and they provided oxygen and service.

Soon the ambulance left with Demarcus, leaving me and Davie with the trap. When the cops came, that's when I left. Davie didn't want me involved, which now I'm very grateful for. However, at the time I wasn't happy because I didn't want to leave Demarcus' side. I was so scared for him. Who would want to harm him like this? The guy didn't rob him or anything. Me and Davie figured someone set up a hit on him. Well, they had greenlit him.

I had no idea how much this incident would affect me till days later. Demarcus was in the ICU for about a week when Davie said we could finally go see him. Me and my family went to see him, and he told us about all the surgery he still had to go through.

#Triggerwarning

They said the bullet was one quarter-inch off from hitting his heart. Any closer, and he would have died immediately.

I will never forget the look on his face. He looked at me and grabbed my hand and said to me, "Get out. It's not worth your life. Listen to me girl: get the fuck out; go live your life and be happy. Stay out of this." I knew this sentiment came from his heart because tears ran down his face.

After more time passed and he was doing better, Demarcus packed all his stuff and moved back to Florida. Things were never the same after he was gone. I'll never forget how those guys tried all they could to be a help to my family. We even lived in that trap house at one point. I was forever grateful for the local dealers because they had saved my life in more than one way. I never got to thank them. Every hood nigga isn't a bad nigga. There are some gems out there.

Prayer for my Enemies

Dear Father God,

I come to you with my knees bent and my heart open. I need your guidance and your understanding. There are those who aim to hurt me and to mistreat me. Father, help me to love past what they have done against me. Help me find forgiveness in my heart even when I feel they don't deserve it. Help me to stay humble and to stay a shining example of your love before every enemy. Let my love for you, Father, break down these walls so that you may come in. Allow them to seek your love and forgiveness. Help them to see who they are in you, Father. Help them to be blessed and safe. Even though they slay me, let your grace and mercy cover them. I am grateful for every enemy because they give me another chance to lead people to you, Father.

Father, show me every enemy no matter how great or how small. Lead me, Father, through the dangerous valleys and the high-up mountains of life. Father, save me for your glory, save my enemies for your glory.

I am your child. I will listen to your voice.

I commit to serving you, despite my circumstances. I will reach out to you in my time of persecution and trust that your will be always present in my life and the lives of those who aim to kill me. I will ask your angels to camp around me in my darkest moments.

I do trust you, heavenly Father. I ask that you change my enemies' hearts and renew their minds.

In Jesus' holy name.

AMEN

Falling Love

I had been having issues in my seven-year relationship, and I could feel things were coming to an end. So I began seeing a gentleman we will call Eric. Eric was a fine and sexy guy; he always said and did the right things. He struggled with day-to-day issues that don't bother most people but were bad for him because he had served in the military and now suffered from PTSD. He had some slight health issues which I definitely overlooked because of my own shortcomings. I had so much on my plate and deserved to have someone love me.

Many nights, I would leave my house and go to his apartment. It was a relaxing environment to be in. We would often cook dinner and watch *Spongebob Squarepants* together.

We both had our moments when we just both were sick of our situations, but I always felt that Eric was faithful and was feeling me. His mouth would say it, and his body would, too, in the times we were intimate. I loved how he loved me. It made me feel special and that someone was seeing me. It was all wrong, but getting the love I lacked felt 'way better. I had been helping him get to work each day after his car broke down. The more I helped him with this and other things. the more I felt needed, and the more I would tell myself it was right.

I had noticed some suspicious little things here and there in his house but would often choose to ignore all the glaring warning signs. I didn't want to stop—but I didn't want to feel hurt either. So, one night when he went to the gym and left me at his place, I thought it would be the perfect time to snoop around and see what he was doing when I wasn't around. Of course, I am a mini investigator and I went around the house reading emails and seeing what I could find.

I ended up in the kitchen, where he had papers piled up on the bar. As I shuffled through this stack, I found a check for $1,000 dollars from a female. Now I was scared I was going to find out more—but I was determined to find out more. I took a deep breath and continued my mission. I soon found another check from another woman, this one for $300.

I had met his mother, and it wasn't her name on the checks. No, it was clear he had various females helping him pay his bills. At that moment, I felt like a fool for thinking he would be loyal to me because of all I had given him.

With my interest completely piqued, I decided to go into his bedroom and get on his computer. I had the sense I would get my answers there, even though I knew he had no Facebook or other apps—or at least that's what he'd told me. I turned on the computer and went to his history because I needed answers. Soon, I found his email and all his pages where he went by various names, none of them his own.

Now I was furious—seeing red—because now I knew everything was one big lie. He had been using me the entire time for sex and for perks. I couldn't believe the hoops I had jumped through for his benefit!

Eventually, I came across letters from a girl in Florida. It seems he had dated her on and off and had recently gone to visit her. I knew because that was the weekend we didn't spend together. Then, as I started digging deeper, I found another email from an older woman who was definitely in love with him. She talked about all the money she had sent him and how he never spent time with her. She pledged to him that she was gonna divorce her husband if that would make Eric happy.

I just couldn't believe any of it! He'd played me like a fool this entire time. So I gathered all my stuff and gathered the information so I could confront him when he got back from the gym. I sat on the couch, just crying silently, zoned out, feeling my mind breaking. I couldn't breathe, I couldn't focus.

See, in my life when trauma would happen, I would go into survival mode. Get what I deem necessary out of the person. Because before I fight with you, I'm going to know the truth. Even if I have to hurt you to get it. This side of me is dark and very dangerous. I don't think things through, and I don't focus on the outcome; I just focus on seeing that the other person feels my pain by any means necessary. I was bent on getting my answers.

I kept looking out the window so I could see as soon as he pulled up. I was full of anger and pain, heartbreak and defeat, shock and betrayal. I wanted to know the truth.

Finally, he got home, came up the stairs, and unlocked the door. I saw him and was quiet. He immediately noticed how my energy was. He asked, "Are you okay? You look upset,"

I looked down the floor and tried to stay level headed, but I could feel my anger rising to the top. So I turned and faced him. I looked deep into his eyes and asked, really easy like, "Are there other women you are seeing? Tell me the truth because if you lie it will only make things worse."

He completely stopped everything he was doing and looked at me and said, "I ain't dating other people, and, if I was, how would it matter? You already have a man."

I went quiet for a minute, and then I told him that I had found out everything and that there was no need to lie to me because I'd seen his mail and his email. I pleaded with him to tell me the truth, and he still dismissed me.

By this point, I was standing in the kitchen, facing him. I grabbed a glass as if I was going to drink. I looked him in the eyes again and asked him loudly, "Just tell me the truth; I just want answers."

He looked at me and said, "I don't know what to tell you. You shouldn't have gone into my stuff. You looked for something, and you found it." He dismissed my questions and dismissed my heart. I was angry…

I paused, and then I took a breath and flung the glass right at his head. If he didn't care about me, I didn't care about his ass.

Soon it took off like a flight. We both began fighting, him trying to hold me down, me grabbing all the glass I could, throwing it at his head and body.

Before you knew it, we were tussling on the floor. I had enraged him and got him super pissed off. He was trying to get control; I wasn't about to give up control.

He body slammed me, and I landed on some of the glass I had previously thrown.

He screamed, "You gotta get out my house!"

I screamed in reply, "I'm not going nowhere!" I was so mad that I went crazy, biting and kick him. I even kicked him in his balls, and that put him in pain quickly.

I tried with all my might to stay there and get my answers one way or the other. But he grabbed my arms and pulled me across the floor as fast as he could, dragging me to the front door where all my belongings were—with me kicking and screaming all the way. "Muthafucka! I ain't going nowhere! You're going to give me my answers! I want the truth asshole!"

Then he punched me in my chest, and I felt myself choking; I started coughing. But I continued to fight.

We were at the front door, and he was pushing me out the door. I turned around and slapped him three times in rapid succession.

He yelled, "Get the fuck out my house! You have lost your mind." And—guess what: he definitely was right. I had lost my mind in more ways than I knew.

Soon he had pushed me down onto his front step. A neighbor looked out from his door and saw us engaged in a battle. Eric yelled out to his neighbor, "Hey, call the police! she is trippin'!"

I told the neighbor, "Close your door! He doesn't need any help with his cheating ass!"

The neighbor went back into his home and called the police anyway.

Eric and I continued to tussle and argue, and now people were coming out of their apartments because of all the commotion. Eric grabbed my arms—to stop me from leaving before the cops came, I guess—and he ended up pushing me down the steps.

Once I realized I was falling down the flight of stairs with enforced metal on their edges, I knew at that moment I was never going to get answers, and the answers no longer mattered—because, if a man could throw me downstairs, there was no way he ever really loved me.

Eric went back into his house, then came back outside and threw my things out of his apartment onto the stairs. He was yelling for me to leave, but all I could do was sit and cry.

The police arrived and asked him what he wanted done. He quickly said, "I just want her to leave."

The cop came down to me and looked at all my things everywhere. He asked me, "Ma'am, are these your things?" I nodded yes. He then asked me if I broke anything and I showed him my scratched-up back and arms. He asked if I wanted to press charges. I shook my head no.

As I sat there and thought about everything that had happened, I felt so little and so unloved. I felt like trash he had just discarded. I wasn't even important enough to him for him to give me the simple truth. As I was lying there on those steps, my pain spoke loud.

The officer helped me pick up all my stuff. I sat on the stair, putting various things back into my bag. At that very moment, the officer said to me, "If that's love, young lady, you don't need it; you need to go home to your family and never come here again. This ain't love. Remember that love—true love—doesn't hurt."

I'll never forget him and how kind he was to me. Sometimes I think of him. He truly helped me that day.

Once the officer helped me put all my stuff in the car, he patted me on the back and said, "It will be okay, darling. There are more fish in the sea. You just caught the wrong one." He smiled and watched me crank my car up to leave.

As my music in the car came on, it was playing Usher's "Moving Mountains." I definitely felt that this relationship was a mountain to me. No matter what I did or said, at the end of the day, I wasn't important to Eric; I was just a woman with perks. Perks that only benefited him. I decided that, from that moment on, I deserved to be cherished and loved. and. if I couldn't get that from you, I wouldn't even have time for you. I'm more than just a perk. I'm worthy of greatness. I deserve it.

Prayer for Guidance

Dear Father,

I come before you with what's in my heart. I want to know my path and where to go on this road called life. I want to know my path and its turns. I want to be able to see the enemy before he strikes. Father, I want clarity in every area of my life. Help me understand your will and your way. Help me to receive revelation from reading your mighty word. Father, let my bible be my road map. Help me navigate the stormy seas and to see even in the dark. Keep my mind fixed on you. Keep my word to hear your instructions. Take my mind and quiet it. Father, give me wisdom to gain knowledge that will aid me on my journey. Father, do guide me till I reach my heavenly home one day. Protect me, Father. Please guide my family and their decisions. Keep us always in your heart. Let all our life glorify you, Father. I am listening, and I am ready to hear.

amen

Bittersweet Dad

When I was a kid, my childhood was actually pretty great, and my mom's and my dad's family were close to me. Before my grandfather passed away, the family was so strong and stable, but, once he was gone, I started to see the cracks showing. He was the glue.

Well, around this time, my mother met a man named Tee. He was very kind and pleasant and very in love with her. He had everything she wanted, and he found everything he wanted in my mom. I remember how he would always kiss my mom and be so loving, even bring her flowers when she was down. He really felt she was the love of his life and vice versa. Soon, he asked her to marry him, and I was super excited because my mom needed help with my baby sister. This would be great.

Tee was very interested in teaching me and my sister all he could. He taught us games and how to play sports and how to draw and how to write. He was a great painter and drawer. He taught me all he could. I remember once I said, "I wish I could play piano," and he went out and got me an organ to play. I loved that thing, and he sat with me and helped me learn how to play it.

One of my favorite memories is of the time he got me and my middle sister our first bunk beds. We were so excited. I got the top, and she got the bottom. My sister and I also got our first Cabbage-Patch-Kids, Feivel-the-Mouse, and Jem-and-the-

Hologram dolls all from Tee. He loved to spoil us. He even took us on trips to King Dominion Amusement Park in Virginia and Carowinds Amusement Park in Charlotte, North Carolina. He also would take us to see the fireworks on every major holiday.

All our memories were beautiful and full of love. We all did everything together. Even our Christmases were legendary. We would always have toys stacked from under the Christmas tree all the way to the middle of the living-room floor. Most times me and my sister would give toys to other kids who had no toys because we had so many.

But little did my mom and her daughters know that trouble was around the corner for us all. The depth of the darkness coming for us was going to take us to places we never wanted to be. Would love survive through it, or was love just not enough?

Our stepdad was always a very calm and non-confrontational individual. He would often leave the house, gathering things to sell at the local flea market. He was extremely good at selling and restoring things. The flea market was one of the extra-income things, outside of his regular job, that he did to provide for us. For years he would bring stuff in and out the house. We would keep what my mom liked and let go of the rest.

As time progressed, we noticed certain small changes at first. He normally would do flea markets on Saturday, but now he was going away the entire weekend. My mother and he began to argue nonstop. Me and my middle sister knew there was trouble in paradise. Mom would always cook dinner, and we all would sit and eat together. However, now he would make a plate and leave or he wouldn't come home at all. My mom knew something was really wrong but she continued to fight for her marriage.

Soon Tee stopped paying bills on time or wouldn't pay bills at all. I'll never forget all the times I kept a screwdriver and hammer in my bookbag in case we got home to find they had padlocked the door because of evictions; me and my sister could still break in and do our normal routine. I can't tell you how many times this took place. It was embarrassing, and it was so sad and draining. Everyone at school from our neighborhood would laugh at us.

We all knew something was wrong, and eventually my mom no longer trusted Tee with our bill money; she would try and handle bills herself. I'll never forget the many times we moved: over 36 times, and most were because of evictions. We literally were hanging on by threads.

My mother got to the point where she wouldn't sleep with my stepfather any longer. She would sleep alone in her room or come and sleep with me and my younger sister.

We knew things were getting worse. I knew mom found out about other women he was seeing, and eventually we found out about Tee's drug habit. He really didn't care who he hurt or what he had to do to get his fix. From the dad we had grown to love, he became a sign of our pain.

*****

#Triggerwarning

My sister and I remember very vividly a circumstance where our house got shot up from a drive-by shooting.

Our stepfather, Tee, had got us into this beautiful house on Peyton Street in a good neighborhood. It was our first real home. It was brick and had three bedrooms. Me and my sister had a front yard and back yard with a fence, and our bus would pick me up each morning right from our yard. My sister could walk to her school. It was a perfect first home. We all loved it. My mom adored the big kitchen and cozy living room. Every day seemed like a great day in that house.

I even remember having a crush on the brothers who stayed next door to us. I was in love with Roni, but he was too old for me—though, trust me, a sister could dream. Tee never let boys around us; he wasn't okay with that. He intended to keep us holy, wholesome virgin girls till we got married one day. I'm grateful he was that way.

We knew Tee was still up to his regular tricks, and my mom was stressed, like usual. He was always selling stuff and bringing crap into the house. It drove her crazy unless he had stuff we could use in the house. I loved all the cool stuff even if it wasn't mine. He used to bring us so many books and magazines. I absolutely loved it. He also brought us toys all the time as well.

This particular day—I will never forget that day for the rest of my life—started out like a regular Saturday. Me and my sister were in our bedroom playing, having fun. I remember suggesting to my middle sister that we get up, put away our toys and dolls, and go watch tv. Tee was in the back yard working on his weekly sale stuff, mom was doing work around the house, and my sister Vee went to the kitchen to grab popcorn for us.

I decided I would go look out the front door and window to see if Roni was in his yard. I just loved seeing him. I approached slowly, and I noticed a white van speeding up the hill from the old apartment complex across the street. I knew something was off because of the way they were driving.

The van sped up, and a man wearing a white shirt and khaki shorts pulled out a rifle and started shooting toward our house. I ran, ducked down, and was going toward the hallway when I heard glass breaking in the living room and bullets coming through the wall. I screamed loudly, "They shooting! Get down; they shooting!" I was terrified.

Immediately I remembered my sister and ran to the kitchen to see if she was all right. As I got to the kitchen, the shots kept coming, and my sister started ducking. We both saw a bullet go directly above her head, less than an inch from her skull, into the kitchen wall in front of us. I'll never forget the looks on our faces. If she had stayed there a second later, she would have died; the bullet would have gone into her head. All we could do was hold each other.

I crawled back into the living room. The guy had stopped shooting and gotten back into that weird-driving white van. They sped off in a hurry. I will never forget that.

The cops were called, and they came to the house about an hour later. They dusted and took the bullets out of the walls. They also set an appointment for me to come down and look through their books to see if I could recognize anyone that could have done it.

I honestly was scared and thought *What if they come back and finish what they started?* So I gave the cops a bum steer and chose who I thought it could have been, but I wasn't sure, so I knew they couldn't use my identification.

I remember how scared me and my mom and sister were after that shooting. It could have killed my sister. It could have killed everyone. A couple weeks later, my mom heard from someone in our neighborhood that my stepdad owed money to a drug dealer, and the dealer was pissed and shot up our house as a warning to Tee. We really didn't know if it was true but I knew that, often, if the streets tell you something, it's usually true. The streets never lie.

We never found out who had done it. And our hopes of a happy safe home left us on that day. Home wasn't sweet anymore.

*****

I believe this moment was a pivotal turning point in the relationship between my mom and stepfather.

We moved into another house, and it had a storage shed in the yard where Tee kept his tools. Me and my sister would often go out there to play, even though Tee warned us not to go in the shed. So what did we do? We went to the shack.

One day when I was outside playing with my pet turtle, I decided I wanted to find something he would like to eat. In the shack with all the tools, I noticed a clear plastic bag with syringes in it. I was shocked because no one in the house had any health issues that required needles. I ran and grabbed my mom. She stared at the bag with sadness and heartbreak. I believe this was the moment she determined she needed to get tee help and that she and her girls would need to finally leave.

At that moment, she was in a survival mode; she only cared about protecting herself and her daughters. She was at war with a drug addict. She was at war with the love of her life. Her heart was in shambles, and she was tired of all the problems and drama. She went on a mission to get Tee help from the church through therapy and in getting him into a treatment program.

After the treatment program, Tee would get better at home but slowly slip back into his old ways. I remember my mom trying everything she could to salvage the broken life she now had.

I will never forget when he started stealing items even from us. If he was really hard up for money, he would sell our mom's towels to his family members. We would often see items from our house in their houses. We would tell them, and they would always say they didn't know where the items came from. It was very painful and embarrassing.

I remember once we had all got new dresses and shoes and jewelry for the choir anniversary for the kids at the church. We had picked out all-white dresses from the second-hand store. We left everything laying out in our bedrooms so it wouldn't get wrinkled. After rehearsal at church, we headed home. Once we were back in the house, something immediately looked different. We were missing chairs, plates, and pots and pans—but most of all we were missing our clothing and shoes and the blankets off our beds. My tv was even gone. Most of my middle sister's toys were missing. My mom was missing all her jewelry, and so was I. It was such a horrible reminder that we were no longer living with Tee; we were definitely living with a fully functioning drug addict. He completely broke our hearts—especially my sister's; she just was torn up inside so badly.

We felt abandoned and that we no longer meant anything to Tee. We had to find a way out. Soon, the arguments were so bad that Tee wouldn't even come home, which for us was a good weekend because he wasn't fussing and stealing from us.

Then one day he brought all these brand-new computers into the house. I remember mom saying to us, "Don't touch anything because your stepdad may have stolen them from somewhere." And, just like most times, mom's intuition was right. The very next day a police detective came to our house looking for the computers from the Wake Health department. Although we had suspected as much, we were in shock that Tee had stolen from them.

The detective left his card and asked us to call him if Tee came back. But we already knew they would never see those computers again. Tee was into fraud and bad checks and was excellent at making things disappear. No matter what, he always found a way out of the issues he created for himself.

My mom was so exhausted with it all and began to speak to the gentleman next door. She felt she had someone to talk to and confide in. He and his aunt were very kind to us when Tee wasn't at the house. The man would often take my mom places because Tee had made her car undriveable.

Her time with the next-door gentleman was very innocent. He even told our mom, if she left her husband, he would take care of all of us and get us our own place together. My mom truly believed him, and so did I. My sister didn't trust him at all. But mother had said he hadn't lied or treated her wrong and she trusted him. She was going to finally leave Tee and the pain for a new life with her gentleman friend. Little did we know everything was really about to hit the fan. We had no idea where this road was taking us.

One weekend when the house was quiet and we were all doing whatever you do on Saturdays, Tee came in the house, bringing junk and being very loud and rude to everyone—but mainly to my mother. We always knew, if he started a huge argument, he was only looking for a way out of the house for that night. My mom wasn't even trying to argue because she was exhausted by the entire situation. She really didn't say much at all, but he claimed that she was cheating on him and the house wasn't clean enough. She was telling him she was faithful to him and the entire marriage, and me and my sister knew she was telling the truth, but he wanted to believe whatever lies he had put in his mind.

My mom had plenty of opportunity and space to cheat on Tee, but he was the love of her life, and she wanted no one but him. Now the one thing she never did was the one thing he accused her of. Imagine the love of your life picking on your heart piece by piece till nothing remains. My mom had tried everything to save her marriage, but she was now at the breaking point of no return. This day she finally said that, if he didn't get it together, she would leave him and find someone else.

He went raving mad and threw this crystal bowl into a glass table, shattering everything. The bowl had been a gift from the children she directed in the choir at church. That was the one item she cherished above all others, and he had broken it and the glass table into pieces. I remember her crying as we all helped him clean it up. I told her, "Mama, we got it; just go relax; we are so sorry this happened."

She gazed at the shattered mess and then looked up slowly and said, "He will not abuse me or my girls any longer. I'm done with this marriage—all of it." The look of utter disappointment on her face told me and my middle sister that she was completely done, and, unlike other times, we knew this time was different. She meant it with every fiber of her being.

The very next day she walked over to the gentleman's house next door. She told him and his aunt everything that happened, and they both agreed they would assist her in leaving Tee. My mother felt confident in her decision because she wasn't going to be alone as she had been in her past. WE all decided to move out during the day when Tee wouldn't come in till late. We would pack everything and load up a U-haul and go on to our new life with the aid of mom's gentleman friend.

She had started to become serious about having a relationship with him. However, we didn't know exactly how serious he was about her; today we would see if he came through with his assistance. I remember going over there to check and knocking on the door—but nobody answered. His aunt's car was gone, and his car was in the backyard, but he either wasn't there or was ignoring my knocks.

I told mom, who called over there, and no one picked up the phone. I remember the sadness in my mother's face. Did her gentleman aide abandon her and her kids too?

We eventually realized he was a no-show and decided to move forward without his help and no money. We packed the U-haul full and then took all our furniture and precious memories to a local storage. We kept paying for that storage until eventually we no longer could and then lost everything we ever owned. All our memories are gone. All my grandmother's furniture is gone—all our pictures and books and dolls and tv's, all gone.

The night we moved out, we had nowhere to go, so my mom decided to go to her God aunt Josephine's house. She was kind and opened her living room to us until we could find somewhere else to go.

Eventually, we left there because her husband complained so much about us being there, even when we were not around that much. We only slept there and showered there.

We ended up staying with Josephine's disabled son, Lee. He gave us his entire bedroom, which really was so very kind. We stayed there for a while until he got up and moved back to his mother's house because of money issues.

From there, we moved in with our cousin Paula and her five kids. It was crazy staying there. Never a dull moment, but it was very chaotic, and we really could deal with it well.

Eventually Paula's friend offered to get us a hotel room during the Christmas holiday. So we got our clothes and went to the hotel. We spent Christmas and New

Year's in a hotel. We had no gifts because we had no money. Mom was out of work, and I wasn't old enough to work.

So, once our time was done there, we moved to our cousin Etta's house with her and our two cousins who were married. They really liked us being there. Etta gave us her third bedroom, which she had been using as her storage unit. It even had a toilet in it. We were happy to be safe and just have a warm safe place to be. I slept in the bathroom, and my mom and middle sister lay on the couch and floor.

We all were so sad and depressed because of all the things we had been dealing with. At one point during this ordeal, mom checked out completely. She had become physically sick and wasn't eating and was in severe clinical depression. She was doing the best she could with all she had, but I had to take the reins of responsibility and act as the mother figure till she was better. Little did I know those roles would never really be the same ever again. I never told my father about any of this, worried that I would be taken away from my mother if I did.

We stayed at Etta's for some months, and Christmas rolled around again. The week of Christmas, Etta asked us to leave and take everything. We really had nowhere to go and didn't know what to do or what actually caused her to ask us to leave. I sttill have no clue, even now.

We ended up at the shelter in downtown Raleigh for some months. That experience was just an open door to more crazy stuff. I remember how people treated us, knowing we were homeless. People often looked down on us and felt as if we were dirty human beings or maybe thought we were on drugs or something, but absolutely none of it was true.

Most of the women and kids in the shelter came from abusive and dangerous homes—mostly domestic-violence situations. One lady used to tell us how bad her husband had beat on her and her kids. To her and her family, the shelter was a piece of heaven she had never known.

There were always about six families, all women and children, staying there in increments of three to six months. We all had such different stories but one thing was absolutely clear, that every single mom there loved their kids with all they had inside them and were fighting to keep us all safe.

My middle sister spent a lot of time in the restroom because it was like a locker room. We could talk and listen to music without distraction. It was our peaceful place. Our mom would go to work, and we would go to school every day and then go home to the shelter. I often told my friends in class that I worked there,so as not to create issues for our mother.

Once there was a bad snow blizzard, and the staff at the center couldn't get there to feed us or the other homeless who were depending on the meals. Well, true to her nature, my mom rose to the occasion and suggested that, if we just broke into the kitchen, she would cook for everyone. And, just like that, our entire floor was on a mission. Our roommate and her son broke into the lock and got it open quickly. Mama had me and my middle sister help her get things together and gave everyone jobs to do, and, before you know it, we had a Thanksgiving-style breakfast of champions. My mom was not just our star but everyone else's, too. I was so glad she was mine.

Soon a TV crew was called, and we were on the news because of the citation: Leaving mothers and kids alone in a facility with no food and no staff was definitely newsworthy. One of the mothers also told them about the cars that had been donated but which no one had received.

It was crazy at the center after that. My mom would do her best to make it to work every day. The center had crazy rules, so it was hard to work and still get your kids together by a certain time every day. My mom had already lost one job while we were there because of the ridiculous rules. We longed for home.

Finally, after my mom had saved up some cash she found a long house on Cook Street. She could afford it, and I could get a job and assist her with things. However, the day we left the shelter was bittersweet because all those women and kids had become like family. We knew we would not see those folks ever again, but we often prayed they would find a home of their own, also.

So we finally got into the place. It was a one-bedroom shotgun house. (A shotgun house is a narrow, rectangular house, usually no more than about 12 feet wide, with rooms arranged one behind the other and doors at each end of the house.) There was a living room, a kitchen, a bathroom, and a bedroom. It wasn't much, but it was ours and we were so grateful for it.

Life was so different without Tee and all the chaos. We had even stopped going to church much after everything happened. We had just been struggling so much and couldn't dedicate ourselves like we wanted. Tee had created so much trauma for us, and, till this day, me and my sister often wonder if he even remembers everything he took all of us through, especially our mother. She loved him with everything she had, and even that wasn't enough.

My mom suffered terrible depression after her divorce. She never married anyone ever again. She found peace in the life she had created for herself and her girls. She was serious about not having trauma affect us anymore if she could help it, but little did she know things would never really be the same. Life had dealt her a solid blow; she came up fighting for herself and her kids. God brought us through so much, and we were grateful.

Soon we would move up to better locations out of that shotgun house. Each time doing better and better. If Tee taught any of us anything, it was to hustle and to stand on your own. Now, it wasn't easy, and it wasn't what we truly wanted, but it was a start in the right direction.

Last Prayer: Thanks

I have been through so much, Father, and I am still alive.

I am grateful for the life you have blessed me with. Father, your love is everything to me. Please don't stop loving me. I'm grateful for every person who was a part of my life, whether good or bad. Everything led me to this moment right here.

I am blessed that you have put so much love around me. Every day, I see your grace and mercy through others and myself. I want to always have an attitude of gratitude. Father, bless those who have hurt or harmed me. Forgive them, Father, for they know not what they do. Help them to get closer to you and allow the spirit of forgiveness to be their portion. Bless my enemies, known and unknown.

I am thankful for my family and thankful for their love. Father, please protect them in every way. Family is our greatest gift in the world.

Father, heal those who are hurt and in great pain; let them know you are indeed the greatest healer. Father, forgives our every sin and let us learn from them. Father, push us to be a godly example to those who are around us or look up to us. Let us pattern our life after your word.

Father, send comfort to those who are broken. Give them peace in their trials.

Comfort them on their journey of healing and redemption. Allow them to feel your love in every way.

Father, allow us to always follow you. Let us not be led astray by our thoughts and those we have around us. Father, allow healing to be our portion. Anoint us with your blood that was shed for our sins; let it cover us. We are nothing without you, Father. We are lost without your instruction. Guide our every step and every thought. Let us not be weary in well doing. Let us not give up on ourselves. We deserve love.

Father, teach us the lessons we need so that we may see your glory in everything. Give wholeness to us that we may not remain broken. Mend our hearts and our minds. Heal our body and soul. We are grateful for all you have done for us. We are blessed that our life and testimony can be a lesson to those who will hear us. We are not alone, for your love envelopes us. We are your children, saved by grace. Keep us in your holy word, and keep our minds clean and renewed.

The pain is only a part of our story, but we are greater than that which tried to take us down. We praise you, Father, for clarity and direction. We praise you for confirmation. We bless you for healing hearts and minds. Father, do send your angels to us to help keep and protect us, your vessels.

Lord, let your light shine on us and shine on others. We are nothing without you. We are forever grateful for your care and tenderness. Give us complete peace. We are so much greater than our circumstances. We shall be healed in Jesus' holy and blessed name. We are grateful for your will and your way. Let us never forget where we came from. Help us to stay humble and gracious at all times.

Thank you for saving us even when we did not deserve it. We are your children, and we desire to be most like you, Father. I shall keep your name in my mouth at all times. We shall always be your children. We praise you, holy Father, for it all.

Father, be praised at all times for the life you have given me. Keep me always in your will and your way. When I feel lost, keep me on the narrow road. I will praise you at all times. You are the greatest love of my life. Thank you.

AMEN